WILLIAM
PENN
FOUNDER OF PENNSYLVANIA

WILLIAM
PENN
FOUNDER OF PENNSYLVANIA

by Barbara A. Somervill

Content Adviser: Craig Horle, Ph.D.,
Director and Chief Editor,
Biographical Dictionary of Pennsylvania Legislators

Reading Adviser: Rosemary G. Palmer, Ph.D.,
Department of Literacy, College of Education,
Boise State University

COMPASS POINT BOOKS MINNEAPOLIS, MINNESOTA

Compass Point Books
3109 West 50th Street, #115
Minneapolis, MN 55410

Visit Compass Point Books on the Internet at *www.compasspointbooks.com*
or e-mail your request to *custserv@compasspointbooks.com*

Editor: Julie Gassman
Page Production: Noumenon Creative
Photo Researcher: Svetlana Zhurkin
Cartographer: XNR Productions, Inc.
Library Consultant: Kathleen Baxter

Art Director: Jaime Martens
Creative Director: Keith Griffin
Editorial Director: Carol Jones
Managing Editor: Catherine Neitge

Library of Congress Cataloging-in-Publication Data
Somervill, Barbara A.
  William Penn: founder of Pennsylvania / by Barbara A. Somervill.
    p. cm.— (Signature lives)
  Includes bibliographical references and index.
  ISBN-13: 978-0-7565-1598-0 (hardcover)
  ISBN-10: 0-7565-1598-X (hardcover)
  ISBN-13: 978-0-7565-1788-5 (paperback)
  ISBN-10: 0-7565-1788-5 (paperback)
  1. Penn, William, 1644–1718—Juvenile literature. 2. Pioneers—
Pennsylvania—Biography—Juvenile literature. 3. Quakers—
Pennsylvania—Biography—Juvenile literature. 4. Pennsylvania—History—
Colonial period, ca. 1600–1775—Juvenile literature. I. Title. II. Series.
  F152.2.S66 2006
  974.8'02092—dc22   2005025216

Signature Lives

COLONIAL AMERICA ERA

As they arrived in North America, European colonists found an expansive land of potential riches and unlimited opportunities. Many left their homes in the Old World seeking religious and political freedom. Others sought the chance to build a better life for themselves. The effort to settle a vast new land was not easy, and the colonists faced struggles over land, religion, and freedoms. But despite the many conflicts, great cities emerged, new industries developed, and the foundation for a new type of government was laid. Meanwhile, Native Americans fought to keep their ancestral lands and traditions alive in a rapidly changing world that became as new to them as it was to the colonists.

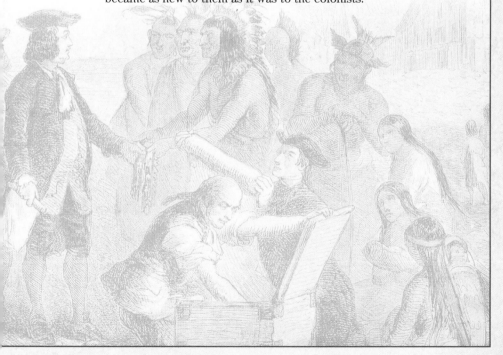

Table of Contents

1 STANDING UP FOR JUSTICE

❧❧❧

It was 1670, and William Penn and William Meade were about to stand trial in one of the most bizarre cases in legal history. It was a time when religious persecution was common, and the two had been arrested for "breaking the king's peace" by preaching to a small group of Quakers on a public street in London, England. Quakerism, which was Penn's and Meade's religion of choice, made the two men targets. Quakers were regularly persecuted for their beliefs.

Before the trial even started, the odds seemed stacked against Penn and Meade. In the 1600s, defendants were not allowed to have lawyers, so they faced the judges alone. To make matters worse, the man who filed charges against the pair also served as one of the judges.

Englishman George Fox had tired of Christians who preached one way and lived another. In 1652, Fox founded a new religion, called the Children of the Light. Fox based his preaching on simple worship, honesty, and equality. Fox's followers attended meetings at which they hoped to find "inward light." His Society of Friends became known as Quakers. The name "Quaker" has two possible sources. Some claim that followers "quaked" when they experienced the "inward light." Others say that Fox warned a judge that he should "tremble (quake) at the word of the Lord."

Things began badly when Penn and Meade entered the courtroom with their hats on. It was against their Quaker religion to remove hats in front of authority, but the judges saw this as a sign of disrespect. Court officers forcibly removed them. But then the bailiff told them to put their hats back on. So they did—only to have the judges accuse them of failing to respect the courts. The judges issued Penn and Meade heavy fines for wearing their hats. They refused to pay and were promptly sentenced to jail time.

After this, a jury of 12 men swore an oath to uphold the law. In the 1600s, juries did not decide if a defendant was guilty or innocent. Instead, they decided if the facts supported the case.

Right after the jury was sworn in, the judges asked Penn and Meade to plead "guilty" or "innocent." Penn asked what the charges were. But the judges refused to provide a written list of the charges until Penn stated his plea. Penn refused to plea until he knew what the charges were. This argument went on until the judges became so annoyed that they put Penn in a room called a bale-dock. The bale-dock was enclosed on all sides except for an opening at the top. The person inside could be heard but not seen. From this room, Penn could not question any witnesses or attack the evidence against him.

Penn reminded the court of the freedoms guaranteed under the Magna Carta. He also warned

In 1215, a group of powerful barons revolted and forced the king to sign the Magna Carta, which guaranteed certain freedoms. This "great charter" had many rights listed, but one of the most important said no man should be jailed without legal reasons.

the judges that they, too, would one day be judged, but their judgment would come from God. Penn's words, however, fell on deaf ears.

The trial was fairly quick since Penn and Meade could not defend themselves. But a defense would not have mattered to the judges. They had already decided on their verdict, and they told the jury to deliver it: guilty on all charges.

Penn warned the jury that if his rights were denied, then anyone's rights could be denied:

> *This I leave to your consciences, who are of the jury (and my sole judges) that if these Ancient Fundamental Laws, which related to Liberty and Property ... must not be indispensably maintained and observed, who can say he hath right to the coat upon his back? Certainly our liberties are openly to be invaded; our wives to be ravished; our children enslaved; our families ruined; and our estates led away in triumph, by every sturdy beggar and malicious informer as their trophies.*

The jury agreed with Penn. They knew that the two men's rights had been trampled on. In spite of the directions given by the judges, the jury found Penn guilty only of preaching, but not of breaking the king's peace. They found Meade not guilty of any charges.

The judges were furious. They sent the jury

back to discuss the case again. This time, the jury found both Penn and Meade innocent. Six times the jury returned a verdict that angered the judges. Jury members were fined. Several agreed to pay the fine, but others refused. So the judges threw the remaining jury members in jail, without food, water, beds, or any comforts. The jurors protested every six hours, determined to be freed by law.

Incredibly, the judges kept the jury members in jail for two months before they were released on appeal. The judges' actions were found to be illegal. This case set a legal precedent about the rights and privileges of juries.

As for Penn and Meade, they went to jail—not for preaching or disturbing the peace, but for wearing their hats in court.

The men were just two of more than 10,000 English Quakers who served jail time for their faith by 1680. Even when Quakers traveled to the New World in the mid-1600s, seeking freedom of religion, they faced persecution once again. The Puritans, who had been abused in England for their beliefs, made laws in their colony of Massachusetts that said all citizens had to be

Many English citizens considered Quakers a threat to their king and government. Because it was against their religion, Quakers would not bear arms against other men and would not serve in the army. It was easy to identify Quakers on the street. They dressed plainly, and their speech used different words and patterns. Quakers were different, and many people feared what they did not understand.

Quaker founder George Fox preaches in a tavern in a painting from the 1700s.

Puritan. Members of other faiths were not welcome.

When the opportunity arose for William Penn to start his own colony in North America, he did not make it a strictly Quaker colony. Instead, he founded a colony based on freedom of religion and fair treatment for all citizens. Penn's plan was simple and very different from what citizens were used to. He would sell plots of land in the colony of Pennsylvania to Quakers or Catholics, Jews or German Protestants. It didn't matter. In Penn's colony, all settlers could practice their own religion without fear. There would be fair laws and fair justice, with a trial by jury. Citizens would have a say in the government, and they could speak out against laws that they believed unfair. They would have to pay taxes for government-run programs, but the taxes would be reasonable.

Attracted by Penn's promises, Quakers from throughout England settled in Pennsylvania. Other groups seeking peaceful lives and the freedom to worship joined them as well: Amish, Catholics, French Huguenots, German Dunkers, Jews, Lutherans, Mennonites, Moravians, and Schwenkfelders. The colony drew settlers from France, Germany, Ireland, and Switzerland—people of all backgrounds brought together by the vision of a faith-filled man.

U.S. President Thomas Jefferson once said that William Penn was "the greatest lawgiver the world has produced; the first, either in ancient or modern times, who has laid the foundation of government in the pure and unadulterated principles of peace, of reason and right."

2 A COMFORTABLE CHILDHOOD

❦

William Penn was born on October 14, 1644, in his father's house in London, England. Luckily for Penn, he managed to survive life in London. Not every child did.

In 1644, London was like most European cities of the time: riddled with disease, too many people, and foul smells. In the 1600s, a traveler smelled a big city before seeing it. London was no exception. Indoor plumbing and flush toilets had not been invented. People used chamber pots as toilets and tossed the contents into the street. It's no wonder most people wore hats, considering what might fly out of second-story windows. The Thames River, passing through the heart of London, served as England's sewer.

Few Londoners had easy access to water, so

William Penn's childhood school, Chigwell Grammar School in Wanstead, Essex, England bathing was, at best, a yearly event. Most people didn't wash their bodies or their clothes. Those who could afford to, covered their body odor with perfume. Toothbrushes and toothpaste did not exist. Not surprisingly, a Londoner's smile often revealed brown, rotting teeth or no teeth at all.

The Penn family, however, lived a fairly comfortable life for the times. William's father was a sea captain, also named William Penn. William's mother was Margaret Jasper Vanderschuren, daughter of a merchant from the Netherlands and widow of a Dutchman.

Admiral Sir William Penn (1621–1670)

The British naval system allowed captains to keep part of any treasures they captured. Serving the government of the times, the senior William Penn sailed the seas and collected his fortune. He was politically smart, and his loyalties shifted with the winds of power. When King Charles I ruled, Penn supported Charles. When Oliver Cromwell rose to power, Penn shifted his loyalty and became Cromwell's sea general. In addition, his family, like most English families, chose to practice Puritanism, the chosen religion of Cromwell's government.

As sea general, Penn helped capture Jamaica in 1655. This Caribbean island had been filled with pirates and all the trouble that pirates brought. Delighted to have the Jamaican problem under control, Cromwell rewarded Penn by giving him Macroom Castle and its lands in Ireland. Macroom had been the site of a major battle between Cromwell's forces and King Charles' army. The castle was a fortress that protected the local village and countryside. Macroom was large enough that Penn could rent out much of the land to tenant farmers, and the rent he received helped support the family. The family did not live at the castle themselves until 1658.

At home in London, Margaret cared for her growing family. When William was a year old, Margaret gave birth to a second son, Richard. A daughter named Margaret was born six years later.

> *A civil war ripped England apart from 1642 to 1651. Conflict started when King Charles I came to power in 1625. He believed that kings got their right to rule directly from God. The powerful English legislature, called Parliament, disagreed. When the Puritan-led Parliament tried to control the king, war broke out. The king's army battled the Parliament's army. In 1646, the Parliament's army under Oliver Cromwell took over the government. From then until his death, England's rule fell to Cromwell, Lord Protector of England. Parliament members tried Charles I for treason and sentenced him to death in 1649.*

During his lifetime William Penn lived in several different English cities.

During most of William's childhood, his father sailed the seas. The family moved to Wanstead, near London, and William went to school in nearby Chigwell. Although rarely home, Penn's father directed young William's education. He hoped the boy would become both a gentleman and a shrewd businessman. William would eventually be responsible for managing the family's money, so he studied math. He also learned the classics, such as Latin and Greek.

Once William turned 12, he left school and was taught by a tutor. As in most lessons of the day, religion was a common topic of discussion. Young William was described as a sensitive, somewhat spiritual child. He claimed God visited him in his dreams.

When Cromwell died in 1658, his oldest son, Richard Cromwell, took on the job of Lord Protector of England. After two years, the political winds shifted again, and Richard was forced to resign. Charles II had been in exile in Holland since his father, Charles I, was executed in 1649. Upon his return to London in 1661, he was crowned king and set up his court. Admiral Penn immediately swore his complete loyalty to the king and was knighted.

King Charles II (1630–1685)

Around this time, young William arrived at Oxford University to attend Christ Church college. The young spiritual boy had grown into a somewhat stubborn young man. At Oxford, William talked with Thomas Loe, a Quaker preacher whom William had met as a boy. William found himself drawn to the simple, honest Quaker faith. He admired Quaker principle, but he had no intention of living without his daily luxuries, as the Quaker religion required.

The change from the Cromwell government to the King Charles II government was soon felt at Oxford. At school, church services were part of the daily studies. With the new king came a change from Puritan services to Anglican services. The Anglican services had too much pomp and ritual to suit William. He refused to go to church services and was fined. William preferred Quaker meetings, which were plain, yet thoughtful.

William's curiosity about the Quaker faith grew. The religion appealed to him because it avoided the punishing attitudes of the Puritans and the overly fancy rites of the Anglicans. The Quakers offered a peaceful, kindly approach to religion. Still, he enjoyed the luxuries of his father's money and was too young to take a serious

Puritans took a stern approach to life. They favored strict moral conduct, avoidance of all sins, and extremely simple church services. The Anglicans, in comparison, took an open-minded view of life. They preferred churches decorated with gold and gems, and services featuring music. Anglicans did not want to control people's private lives the way the Puritans did. But both religions tried to force their beliefs on others through military power, legal persecution, and executions of nonbelievers.

Christ Church College at Oxford where Penn attended school as a young man.

interest in the Society of Friends. Besides, the Penn family's welfare depended on being "politically correct," and following the Quaker faith was not socially acceptable.

In 1662, William was expelled from Oxford for his rebellion. His parents decided to send him to France. Children of wealthy families were often sent on tours of Europe in order to experience the continent's various cultures. But a lengthy trip in Europe was also a popular means of getting an unruly child out of the way. Later in life, William looked on this time as being banished from the family—saying he was beaten and whipped by his father because he preferred the Quaker religion. But he exaggerated the situation. He lived quite well in the court of Louis XIV. He loved the velvets, silks, and laces worn by the French nobles, and he soon began dressing like them. The fun and folly of the French court delighted him.

At this time, the French government allowed its citizens freedom to learn about different religions. William was pleased to pursue this freedom. In France, learning about Protestant beliefs was popular, and William attended the Protestant Academy of Saumur. The academy was run by a

The French fashions William admired featured expensive cloth and delicate laces.

famous Protestant preacher, Moise Amyraut, who spoke of an "inner light" that led people to God. William admired Amyraut and took the preacher's teachings to heart. Later, his devotion to the Quaker faith and his political attitudes reflected his belief in a guiding inner light.

In 1664, William Penn returned to England an overdressed, pompous young man. He was described as having "a great deal, if not too much, of the vanity of the French (clothing) and affected manner of speech and (walking)." His love of fine clothing and elegant living made his future conversion to the Quaker faith all the more surprising. ॐ

3 PENN, THE QUAKER

Chapter

❧❧

At age 20, William Penn decided to study law in London's legal district. Future lawyers did not go to law school. They studied with working attorneys. These student-teacher relationships usually came about through family friends, money, or political influence. Luckily for Penn, his father had all three.

But events soon arose to change William's plans. A few months after he began his studies, bubonic plague broke out in London. Doctors and religious leaders fled the city, leaving the sick to tend themselves. Penn noticed that the only people willing to care for plague victims were Quakers. Regardless of the danger to their own health, hundreds of Quakers fed and bathed the sick and buried the dead with dignity. The Quakers' kindness impressed him deeply.

At age 22, William Penn hired an artist to paint his portrait as a soldier.

Victims of the plague were discovered in the streets of London.

Also around this time, war broke out between Britain and the Netherlands. To help with the war effort, Admiral Penn asked William to work on his staff. But the senior Penn had no intention of exposing his son to battle, so young Penn became a messenger between the admiral and King Charles II.

William worked directly for his father, a situation that was not always comfortable. The relationship between father and son had been strained because of William's interest in the Quakers. But the war kept him too busy for religion. And having been thrown into the company of British nobles and government leaders, William was impressed by his close connection to wealth and power. Also, while Quakers avoided showy clothes, no one dressed more fashionably than young William Penn. It seemed he had put his interest in the Quakers behind him.

When William's job as a military messenger ended, he returned to his law studies. But the plague made living in London too dangerous. He left the city and headed to Ireland. There he would manage his father's Irish estates.

The Penns farmed some of the land at Macroom Castle.

In 1665, panic swept through London's streets as the bubonic plague appeared. People scrawled prayers in doorways: "Lord, Have mercy on us." Behind those doors, the sick lay in agony as black patches erupted on their skin. Their glands swelled, vomiting followed, and soon, death came. In the streets, wagons passed each morning with drivers calling, "Bring out your dead." Families deposited bodies of loved ones on the pile to be buried in mass graves. When winter finally brought an end to the epidemic, more than 70,000 people had died in London alone.

It became William's job to oversee the planting, tending, harvesting, and sale of crops, as well as the sheepshearing and cow milking. William collected rents from the tenant farmers on the castle's land and saw to their needs. The Penns owned the cottages that the farmers lived in, and William had to make sure roofs were secure and buildings well-maintained. The stone walls that separated the fields needed yearly repair. Managing Macroom required daily attention and plenty of work.

But Penn grew bored with overseeing the farms and tenants of Macroom Castle. He needed some excitement in his life—and he soon got it with a mutiny at Carrickfergus, a port city in Northern Ireland. British soldiers stationed there had gone nine months without pay. In their anger and frustration, they took control of Carrickfergus Castle. The king sent Lord Arran to deal with the soldiers. Young William Penn fancied he'd like a bit of soldiering himself, so he volunteered to help Lord Arran.

The mid-1660s was a difficult time for London. In addition to the plague, the city suffered the Great Fire of 1666. The fire started on September 2 in a baker's house on Pudding Lane. The wind carried the fire from house to house. Because there were no professional fire departments at the time, bucket brigades sprang up to douse the flames. Still, by the time the fire burned itself out, more than 75,000 people were homeless. While the Penns' home saw no damage, about 13,200 houses and 87 churches were destroyed citywide.

A painting from the early 1900s shows Carrickfergus Castle where Penn helped end a mutiny.

The mutiny was put down promptly. Penn decided soldiering suited him quite well, and he arranged for an artist to paint his portrait in full armor. This painting shows Penn as a glorified soldier, a very different picture of how he appeared later in life.

Having given up being a lawyer, Penn now planned to be an officer. Most officers did not earn their ranks—they bought them. So Penn asked his father to buy him a commission in the army and a company of foot soldiers. Admiral Penn rejected this idea and ordered William back to his work running Macroom.

One September day in 1667, Penn headed for town to buy some new clothes. He dressed in his finest silks and soft woolens, plopped his wig on his head, and strapped his sword at his waist. He went to a clothing store run by a Quaker woman. Seeing the woman, Penn was reminded of what he had learned

_Macroom Castle
as it looks today_ from the Quaker preacher Thomas Loe and from the
French preacher Amyraut. He recalled how much he
admired the Quakers and their more peaceful, gentler

ways. He talked with the woman about Loe and was surprised to learn that Loe was visiting nearby.

The two men met and talked for hours. Penn began attending local Quaker meetings. He must have looked quite a sight, still in his silks and wigs with his sword at his side. Then one night, soldiers raided a Quaker meeting with Penn in attendance. The soldiers arrested everyone at the meeting, and Penn found himself in jail for a short time.

He finally decided he wanted to become a Quaker. Joining with the Society of Friends was called the convincement. Penn's convincement came in 1667. He was ready to be a Friend, but was he ready to endure persecution? Was he ready to put aside his fancy clothes for plain ones? Was he willing to hold his temper and stubbornness for nonviolent acceptance of life's problems? The answers were "yes"—to everything but the clothes.

4 FAITH ON TRIAL

కుసౠు

For Admiral Sir William Penn, it was a great embarrassment to have his son follow an illegal religion. So in 1668, when 24-year-old William returned to his family's home in London, he asked his son to speak against Quakerism before the king. If William admitted the error of his ways, his father would forgive him. But hot-headed William had no intention of doing what his father asked. So Sir William threw his son out of the house.

Young William didn't suffer much, however. There were plenty of Quakers willing to put him up in their homes. At one point, William stayed with Isaac Penington, a wealthy Quaker from Buckinghamshire. At the Penington home, Penn met Gulielma Maria Springett, Penington's stepdaughter. Guli was open,

William Penn used his time in prison to write about religion.

friendly, and sweet-tempered. She drew others into comfortable conversation and listened to their thoughts. William and Guli fell instantly and deeply in love.

Along with his newfound love for Guli, Penn experienced a deeper devotion to his faith. Penn became very religious and began attacking the beliefs of other religions. He wrote an essay called *Truth Exalted*, in which he praised the "Glorious Light" found by Quakers on the path to salvation. He wrote against the idea of the trinity—a basic belief of Catholic and Anglican teachings—saying that the belief of God as a father, a son, and a holy spirit was false.

Penn's comments insulted the Anglican Church and broke British law. The Anglican bishop of London ordered Penn's arrest and had him imprisoned in the Tower of London. For the second year in a row, Penn found himself in jail. This time, jail was a serious punishment. He was kept in "close confinement," which meant no visitors of any kind. He ate the same food as common prisoners, had little fuel for heat throughout the winter, and could not even see a doctor without special permission. Worse, he could neither write nor receive letters. But Penn wouldn't go back on what he'd said. Penn wrote, "My prison shall be my grave before I will budge a jot; for I owe my conscience to no mortal man."

Penn stayed in prison for seven months. He used his time well, writing pamphlets about religious freedom. His best-known essay on religious tolerance was *No Cross, No Crown*. In it, Penn describes his belief that people should never be persecuted for their religion. He said, "No pain, no palm; no thorns, no throne; no gall, no glory; no cross, no crown."

Soon, Penn was out of prison, but his freedom was only temporary. In 1670, the government passed the Conventicle Act. While this law allowed Quakers and other sects to gather and worship, it limited the group size to no larger than a family plus five others. The government feared that gatherings any larger than this could be plotting against the government.

Once home to royalty, the Tower of London served as a prison for many years.

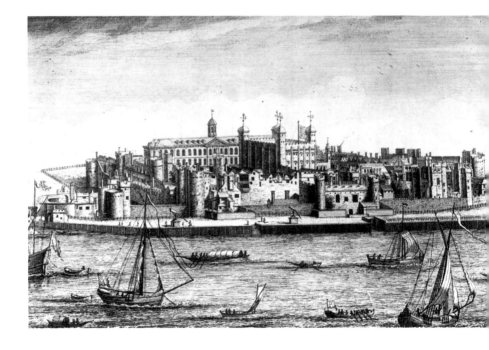

Those who met in larger groups would face consequences, such as jail. Large Anglican gatherings and services, however, were legal.

One day, William Penn headed to Gracechurch Street, London, to attend a Quaker meeting. He found the doors to the meeting hall locked and guarded by soldiers. Penn stood on the sidewalk and began preaching. A small, peaceful group of Quakers gathered around him. Another man, William Meade, also spoke to the group. Soldiers arrested Penn and Meade for conspiring to provoke a riot. The pair quickly found themselves in Newgate Prison, the most horrid jail in England.

Penn was sentenced to prison in Newgate by the lieutenant of the Tower of London.

Following an unusual trial where some of the jury members were jailed, Penn and Meade were found not guilty of the charges. But they still served

jail sentences for failing to remove their hats in court.

The year was a difficult one for Penn. He and Guli Springett had decided to marry, but Penn spent so much time preaching or serving prison sentences that they could not marry until later. In addition, Penn also had family obligations to attend to.

His father, Admiral Sir William Penn, lay dying in his home, weakened by hard years spent as a sailor. He died on September 16, 1670. His military funeral was elegant and quite lavish. A funeral parade passed through Bristol, complete with marching troops. Admiral Penn's armor was displayed, and flags flew representing the three squadrons from his naval career. Then he was buried at St. Mary Redcliffe Church in Bristol.

Young Penn mourned the loss of his father. The two men had never been close, but young William admired his father's accomplishments. He supplied the epitaph for the gravestone:

> *Rather than charging Penn and Meade with violations of the Conventicle Act, the government decided to charge the men for violating the Riot Act because it allowed for more severe punishments. The Riot Act required groups of 12 or more to disperse within one hour of being told to do so by authorities. Punishments under the act allowed for unlimited fines. The law also allowed unlimited jail time, if the violator failed to pay the fine. In contrast, the Conventicle Law had limits on both fines and imprisonment.*

He withdrew, prepared and made for his end; and with a gentle and even gale, in much peace, arrived and anchored in his last and best port, at Wanstead in the County of Essex, the 16th of September, 1670, being then but forty-nine years and four months old. To his name and memory, his surviving lady hath erected this remembrance.

St. Mary Redcliffe Church in Bristol, where Sir Admiral Penn was buried.

After Sir William's death, Margaret Penn kept her home in Wanstead, along with most of Sir William's jewels and a yearly income. Richard Penn, young William's brother, inherited Sir William's swords and guns, cash, and a diamond ring. William's sister, Margaret Penn Lowther, was already married and received only a small amount of money. William, as first son, received everything else.

Sir William's death left Penn a very wealthy man. He inherited all the English and Irish lands and their income, which amounted to about 1,500 pounds a year. This may not sound like a lot of money, but it was a fortune in 1670. At that time, a man who earned 100 pounds a year was well off, and 500 pounds a year made a man rich. In addition, the king owed Sir William—and now his son—several thousand pounds. Penn's fortune was great, and he could now marry his true love. 🔊

The British currency of Penn's time was based on the pound sterling (£), money backed by silver. One pound equaled 20 shillings. Each shilling was worth 12 pennies. A penny could be divided into four farthings (one-fourth a penny) or two half pennies. A guinea equaled one pound plus one shilling, or 21 shillings.

5 A CHARTER FROM THE KING

◦⟨✕⟩◦

Following Quaker traditions, William and Gulielma Springett stated their plan to marry at a regular Quaker meeting. Two members questioned the couple and found no reason to deny the marriage.

The Quaker marriage ceremony was plain. The pair arrived at the meeting hall and sat in silent prayer. The bride did not wear a fancy white dress with yards of lace. No minister read the service, and no oaths were spoken. Quakers did not then, and do not now, swear oaths. This wedding had no flowers, frills, organ serenades, or even gold rings.

Penn and Guli stood before the meeting and spoke of their love and commitment. That was it. They were married. The date was April 4, 1672. Penn believed the marriage was "a match of Providence's

William Penn holds the charter to his colony of Pennsylvania.

making," and Guli "loved him with a deep and upright love, choosing him before all her many suitors."

The Penns made a delightful couple. Guli was young, beautiful, and delicate. Although she dressed plainly compared to the popular fashions of the day, she dressed in luxurious fabrics. She believed in the Quaker faith deeply, so she did not mind Penn's devotion to their faith.

Penn dressed according to his financial status, a wealthy young man from a wealthy family. London's finest tailors made his coats and shirts. He often

An illustration from the late 1600s shows a typical Quaker couple.

wore silk, although he did not have lace at his collar or cuffs.

The marriage was off to a great start. The pair moved into a house in Rickmansworth, Hertfordshire. Here church life provided a variety of activities for the Penns. The couple attended Quaker services and counted the elite of the Quaker faith among their friends. William preached and spread the faith. Guli, along with her fellow Quaker women, cared for the sick and helped the poor. Guli and Penn often invited their Quaker friends to their home for meals. In addition, they read and discussed religious articles with their neighbors. Guli was surprisingly well-educated, considering that girls rarely attended school at the time.

Marriage brought great joy to Guli and Penn, but they also suffered their share of sorrows. After being married a year, Guli gave birth to a daughter, Gulielma Maria, who died as an infant. This was not unusual, since doctors had no vaccinations against whooping cough, diphtheria, mumps, measles, and a host of other diseases. But this did not lessen the pain for Guli and William. Soon, however, Guli was pregnant again.

From 1672 until 1674, King Charles II allowed people to practice their chosen religion. Quakers throughout England—including Penn—attended meetings and preached their beliefs without fear of prison. After 1674, however, Quakers once again faced severe punishments for practicing their religion.

Twins, William and Mary Margaret, arrived in 1674. Baby William died within months of his birth, and Mary survived only a year. The causes of these deaths are unknown. Losing three children so close together distressed the young mother, but her duties as a wife, homemaker, and Quaker kept her occupied. William continued preaching, running the Penn family estates, and caring for his wife.

By 1675, Guli was pregnant again and worried about the child she carried. However, a son they named Springett arrived healthy and thrived, much to Guli's relief.

Soon Penn's duties expanded beyond the borders of England and Ireland. In 1676, he was asked to help

Duke of York (1633–1701)

determine a border of a colony in America. New Jersey Colony had begun to grow in 1664 when King Charles II of England gave the land to his brother, the Duke of York. The duke gave the rights to New Jersey to his friends Lord Berkeley and Sir George Carteret, and the two began colonizing their new land. They granted religious freedom to any Englishmen settling in their land. Anyone "having a good musket … and six months' provisions" got a farm, free for five years.

In 1673, two English Quakers had purchased Lord Berkeley's share of New Jersey Colony. But one of the buyers, Edward Byllinge, went bankrupt. His share was then handled by a group of trustees, including Penn, who would help manage the Quakers' interest in the land. In 1676, the colony was divided into East Jersey and West Jersey. Penn

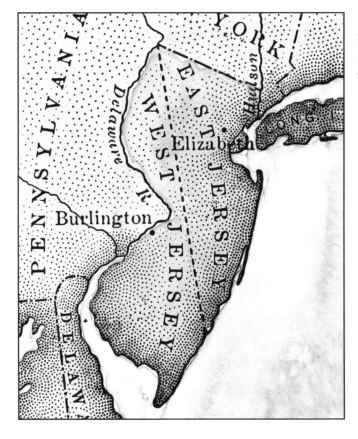

The state of New Jersey was once two colonies: East Jersey and West Jersey.

helped determine the dividing line that stretched between Little Egg Harbor and the Delaware Water Gap. The eastern part of the colony remained under the control of Carteret. West Jersey became the property of Quaker settlers, and Penn helped them set up a legal system and government.

While Penn enjoyed working on the settlement of New Jersey, most of his time was still occupied with running the Penn family estates and preaching. The Irish and English estates provided income from rents that supported William's growing family. The Penns did not live cheaply. They dined on oysters and lobster and drank fine wines and ale. They wore silks, satins, fine wools, and linens. And they filled their homes with elegant furniture.

In 1677, Penn left for a preaching tour in Holland and Germany with George Fox, founder of the Quaker movement. The Quakers held meetings, spreading the word of the Society of Friends. Protestant reforms had brought many changes to Holland and Germany, and Fox and Penn thought they would gain many converts to their faith. They were disappointed. Audiences attended, listened, and then politely refused to join. However, Penn did make important contacts in Europe. A number of Protestant groups he met would later become settlers in his Pennsylvania colony.

When he returned, he set off on a tour of England.

*Persecution
of Quakers
included
unjust trials.*

He preached at Quaker meetings and encouraged
others to look into the Quaker faith. He worked
openly to stop persecution against his fellow Friends.
Meanwhile, at home, the Penn family added another

child, a healthy girl Laetitia, whom Penn fondly called Tish.

Although few Europeans showed an interest in becoming Quakers, Penn was not discouraged and continued writing pamphlets, books, and articles about the Quaker faith. Before he turned 40, he had published more than 50 works.

Although his family was well-supported and he was well-occupied, Penn did not forget about the money King Charles II owed to his family. He repeatedly asked for payment, and the king repeatedly denied his requests. The debt was huge—the equivalent of several hundred thousand dollars today.

By 1680, the king needed solutions for a variety of problems, including Penn's continuing requests for payment. Penn asked the king to grant him a charter to settle a new colony west of the Delaware River in America. The king saw a way to pay off the debt without spending a penny.

Charles II, son of King Charles I, was 30 years old when he was crowned in 1661. As king, Charles faced many problems. His navy lost to the Dutch in a messy war over trade rights in 1664. The Great Plague of 1665 and the Great Fire of 1666 left London a disaster area. In 1667, the Dutch navy burned four battleships in Medway Harbor and took a British ship back to Holland as a trophy. Although the British were glad to have a king again after Cromwell's government, they complained about Charles' policies. England's throne passed to Charles' brother James in 1685, when Charles died.

The process for gaining a charter took months. The council considering Penn's request asked the owners of neighboring colonies what they thought. Although Penn got approval from his old friend the Duke of York, agents representing the owner of Maryland, Lord Baltimore, rejected the idea. They

Charles Calvert, the third Lord Baltimore (1637–1715)

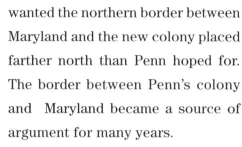

Charles Calvert, the third Lord Baltimore, (1637-1715) was an English noble, a Roman Catholic, and the holder of the Maryland colony charter when Penn founded Pennsylvania.

wanted the northern border between Maryland and the new colony placed farther north than Penn hoped for. The border between Penn's colony and Maryland became a source of argument for many years.

Finally, the council agreed to Penn's charter, and the king signed his name to the document on March 4, 1681. To Penn's dismay, King Charles insisted on naming the colony Pennsylvania, in honor of Penn's father. Penn feared that people would think he named the colony for himself. He tried to bribe the secretary with 20 guineas to change the name, but the secretary refused. He wrote to his friend Robert Turner:

> *This day my country was confirmed to me under the great seal of England, with large powers and privileges, by the name of Pennsylvania; a name the King would give it in honor of my father. I chose New Wales, being, as this, a pretty hilly country.*

Once he had the title to the property, a remarkable 45,000 square miles (117,000 square kilometers) of land, Penn had to encourage people

to move there, set up trade, and develop cities. It was time to "sell" settlers on the new colony of Pennsylvania. ❧

A painting titled The Birth of Pennsylvania, 1680 *shows a seated King Charles II facing William Penn who holds the charter.*

6 PLANNING PENNSYLVANIA

Chapter

ೲೲ

William Penn swung into action. He needed to turn Pennsylvania's forests and meadows into money. Organizing a colony was big business, and Penn worked hard to make Pennsylvania a success. The first thing he did was appoint his cousin Colonel William Markham to serve as his deputy in Pennsylvania. Markham and other agents would manage things there until Penn could go himself.

When Pennsylvania was founded, 11 other colonies already existed. Wages for workers in England had increased, and although persecution of religious groups continued, many Quaker leaders in England encouraged church members to "stand the cross," meaning stay and face persecution. The list of people wanting or needing to move to America

William Penn traveled to the New World on the ship Welcome.

was a short one. Finding colonists would require careful planning.

Penn wrote to the European settlers already living on his land in America. He assured them that they would not lose their farms, and they would live in a land filled with friendship and peace. Penn also wrote to the Indian tribes living in the area. He claimed that he wanted both Indians and colonists to live together peacefully.

Next, Penn addressed his colony's need for a port. His land lay inland, so he would need a way to ship and receive goods. He negotiated with the Duke of York and Lord Baltimore for navigation rights through the Chesapeake Bay and along the Delaware River.

Once this port was ensured, Penn created the Free Society of Traders, a society of businessmen who would establish businesses, shipping, and manufacturing in his new colony. Although Penn did not actually want this society in his colony, Penn's fellow Quakers pressured him to establish it. He saw it as a monopoly on trade.

Next, Penn started laying out a "Frame of Government." He wrote a basic constitution, a legal basis for

While the Free Society of Traders did have some early success with a tannery, sawmill, gristmill, and a glass factory, it soon faced trouble. The charter Penn granted to the society was rejected by Pennsylvania lawmakers. This meant it had no legal right to exist in the colony. It collapsed after about two years.

The Chesapeake Bay, in the middle of Maryland, provided Philadelphia access to the Atlantic Ocean

his free society. Many of the ideas Penn expressed in 1681 would later appear in the Declaration of Independence. One of Penn's ideas reads:

> Men being born with a title to perfect freedom and uncontrolled enjoyment of all the rights and privileges of the law of nature ... no one can be put out of his estate and subjected to the

political view of another, without his consent.

Years earlier, Penn wrote, "True religion does not draw men out of the world but enables them to live better in it." He hoped that his "Holy Experiment"—Pennsylvania—would do the same. It would let people live better, more comfortably, and more safely in their world. At the time, no other government in the world guaranteed the rights and freedoms that citizens in Pennsylvania would enjoy.

Penn's plan for the colony's government called for an appointed governor, a Provincial Council with appointed members, and an Assembly with elected members. Penn hoped that everyone in the colony would serve in the Assembly at some point, but he did not intend for these elected officials to have much power. Instead, the governor and council would make the laws. The Assembly would meet nine times a year to agree to laws suggested by the governor and Provincial Council.

Because Penn and his Quaker friends had suffered for their religion, he wanted his colonists to have freedom of religion. There would be no official religion in Pennsylvania, and there would be no religious persecution.

English Quakers had spent months and years in prison without trials or even a clear statement of charges against them. Pennsylvania would have trial by jury, and the jury's verdict would stand as the final word in court cases. Defendants would be given a clear explanation of the charges against them. Jail sentences would be short for failure to pay debts or while waiting for trials to begin. The death penalty would only be used in cases of treason or murder. Compared to England, where 200-plus crimes carried death penalties, Pennsylvania's justice system seemed extremely merciful.

Slave ownership was written into Penn's first "Frame of Government." Many Quakers saw no problem with slavery. Penn himself owned slaves. Pennsylvania needed cheap labor to become a thriving colony. Penn wasn't squeamish about using slave labor to do it and encouraged the Free Society of Traders to use slave labor.

Penn set to work planning towns and cities in his new colony. He laid out grid patterns of streets and avenues. Every city had wide avenues to prevent fire from spreading as it had in London's Great Fire of 1666. Public parks, squares, and buildings figured in every design. All children would attend a free public school—a building Penn included in his town plans.

Next, Penn reached out to potential colonists. Penn's advertising campaign was a pamphlet called *Some Account of the Province of Pennsylvania.* He encouraged "adventurers" to join him in Pennsylvania. He described the lush forests, clean rivers, abundant wildlife, and opportunities galore. Oddly, Penn had

Penn's "sales" tool: Some Account of the Province of Pennsylvania

SOME

ACCOUNT

OF THE

PROVINCE

OF

PENNSILVANIA

IN

AMERICA;

Lately Granted under the Great Seal

OF

ENGLAND

TO

William Penn, &c.

Together with Priviledges and Powers necef-
fary to the well-governing thereof.

Made publick for the Information of fuch as are or may be
difpofed to Tranfport themfelves or Servants
into thofe Parts.

LONDON: Printed, and Sold by *Benjamin Clark*
Bookfeller in *George-Yard Lombard-ftreet,* 1681.

REDUCED FAC-SIMILE OF TITLE TO "SOME
ACCOUNT."

never been to America, let alone Pennsylvania. His descriptions of rivers, forests, game for hunting, timber for building, and potential crops were just dreams on paper. But he was careful not to claim that he had personal knowledge of the country.

Penn encouraged craftsmen to consider making a home in Pennsylvania. The new colony needed carpenters, masons, smiths, weavers, tailors, tanners, shoemakers, and shipwrights. Penn's pleas succeeded. Nearly half of all new colonists in the 1680s were skilled tradesmen. Another one-fourth set up farms. Pennsylvania was under way.

William Penn's colonists included a wide variety of people. Some had money. Some did not. Penn arranged his land sales so that everyone who wanted to go to Pennsylvania had an opportunity to do so. He negotiated reasonable passage fees with several ships. Adult men and women paid £6 each for travel and food. Travel for adult servants cost £5 each. The charge for children under 7 years old was 50 shillings. Babies still nursing were free. Considering that the average worker earned less than £20 a year, travel costs for a tradesman, his wife, and two children were often more than a year's wages.

It took Penn more than a year to get his affairs in order before he

Europeans with little money tried to improve their lives by becoming indentured servants in America. These servants signed contracts to work for a set period, usually four to five years in Pennsylvania, in return for a ship's passage to America. While under contract, they worked seven days a week doing whatever their "employers" asked. Contract holders provided food, shelter, and clothing in return for about 80 hours of work per week.

could go to Pennsylvania himself. He had to set up responsible people to collect rents, oversee planting, and make needed repairs at the family estates in Ireland and England. Then, just before he was to leave, Penn's mother died, and his mother-in-law, Mary Penington, was dying. Penn had to ensure that his family was well cared for while he was gone.

About this time, Penn's steward, Philip Ford, gave Penn two contracts to sign. One covered a mortgage for 300,000 acres (120,000 hectares) of land to be given to Ford, and the other covered Ford's expenses for work done on Penn's behalf. Penn signed both papers without reading them, or even knowing what they said. At the time, Penn owed Ford an absolute fortune. But Penn had other things to worry about. Sales of land in Pennsylvania went well but did not bring enough income to cover expenses. Penn was a good, honest man, but his business skills were dreadful. Despite his high income, he spent more money than he earned. Like many wealthy people of the time, Penn—who had a great love of luxury—was quick to run up debts and slow to pay. He would live to regret this error.

In the summer of 1682, Penn finally boarded a ship to America. He traveled on the *Welcome* with 100 other passengers. Guli and his children, Springett and Laetitia, remained in England. The Penns were expecting another child, and Guli's health was frail.

William Penn and fellow Quakers journeyed to the New World on a ship named Welcome.

But leaving his family behind was not strange to Penn. After all, his own father had often gone to sea and left his mother to raise the children. In addition, the Penns believed the "Holy Experiment" had to go forth, and Guli was far too sickly to bear the burdens of traveling the Atlantic.

The trip lasted two months. Like most Atlantic crossings in the 1600s, sea travel was unpleasant, food was horrible, and the accommodations were uncomfortable. Many passengers became seasick on the rolling Atlantic waves, and the smell of vomit lingered throughout the ship. An outbreak of smallpox left 30 dead. All in all, it was a typical, ghastly crossing.

Penn missed his wife and family desperately. He was caught between the love of his family and his need to make Pennsylvania pay off. He wrote to Guli, but letters and responses took months to arrive. As an avid writer, Penn had no trouble putting his feelings on paper:

> *My dear Wife and Children.*
>
> *My love, that sea, nor land, nor death itself can extinguish or lessen toward you, most endearedly visits you with eternal embraces and will abide with you forever. And may the God of my life watch over you and bless you and do you good in this world and forever ...*
>
> *My dear wife, remember thou was the love of my youth, and much the joy of my life, the most beloved, as well as most worthy of all my earthly comforts.*

A doting father, Penn also wrote brief notes

directly to his children. He told Springett to "be good, learn to fear God, avoid evil, love thy book, [and] be kind to thy brother and sister."

Dugout homes called cave-dwellings were common among Pennsylvania's poorer colonists.

Penn arrived in Pennsylvania to find clear lines drawn between the wealthy, the merchants, and the poor. Wealthy Pennsylvanians lived in solid homes built with wooden frames that they brought with them from Europe. They also brought furniture, linens, and kitchenware with them. Merchants lived in buildings that combined shops with homes. The store and storage areas took up much of the first floor. Housing was on the second floor or squeezed in the back of the store. The poor lived in log cabins, bark or turf huts, or caves dug into the riverbank, and relied on food offered by the local Indian tribes to survive.

The view of the Delaware River from Pennsbury Manor

Penn's first impressions of Pennsylvania were positive. He praised the soil, clean air, and fresh water. The rivers teemed with fish, and the forests were full of game animals and birds. Penn listed the varieties of trees: black walnut, cedar, pine, cypress, poplar, gum, ash, beech, and several types of oak. Nature provided nuts and wild plums, strawberries, cranberries, and grapes. For the most part, Pennsylvania was everything Penn had promised.

Although he had no family with him, he decided to start building his family mansion and plantation. Called Penn's Palace by some, the new Pennsbury estate would look out over the Delaware River. Penn was drowning in debt, yet he poured money into the building of Pennsbury.

Building began in 1682 and took more than two years to complete. The house had four bedrooms, a nursery, and beds in the attics for servants. The family could entertain in two parlors, a regular hall, and a great hall. Penn furnished his home with elegant, expensive European furniture. He bought the finest linens, tableware, and silverware.

Pennsbury would be the Penn home and a source of income for the family. But he wasn't ready to live there yet, so he hired John Sacher to be his steward and run the plantation. Penn turned his attention to other matters: Philadelphia, the Lenni Lenape, and Lord Baltimore. ❧

7
 Chapter
 PHILADELPHIA, THE LENNI LENAPE, AND LORD BALTIMORE

William Penn's arrival in Pennsylvania meant that several colonial issues could be handled at last. No colony existed without problems, and Penn had plenty to deal with. Demands for his time, opinions, and decisions filled his days. More than anything, he wanted Pennsylvania to be a success, and that could happen only through his own hard work.

The colonists changed Penn's system of government almost immediately. They made the role of Penn's Provincial Council smaller and increased the power of the elected Assembly. If Penn was disappointed in the reaction of his settlers, he hid it well. Besides, there was much more to do.

Elections were held, and the first provincial Assembly met on December 4, 1682. The Assembly

William Penn established an important treaty with the Lenni Lenape Indian tribe.

had fewer representatives than Penn had hoped. However, the representation was enough to guarantee a relatively democratic government. The Assembly granted Pennsylvania citizenship to all settlers living there before Penn's charter took effect. A new law protected citizens' freedom of religious choice. The representatives also set up courts of law and rules of justice, a moral code of behavior, and rules to control businesses.

With the Assembly in place, Penn turned his attention to the city he had named Philadelphia before ever arriving in Pennsylvania. He had spent hours laying out the broad avenues and public buildings. Now, he wanted to watch his model city come to life. Penn hailed his new city:

And thou, Philadelphia, the virgin settlement of this province, named before thou were born, what love, what care, what service and what [effort] has there been, to bring thee forth.

The provincial Assembly set up a list of rules controlling personal conduct as well as business. Most violations carried 5-shilling fines or a punishment of five days in jail with only bread and water. Laws prohibited cursing and swearing, drunkenness, drinking toasts, playing cards or dice, speaking treason, being too loud, or lying about a person or event. Laws also controlled how much an innkeeper could charge for a meal or drink. Inns were required to have stables for horses and at least four beds for travelers. There was even a limit on how long local residents visited a tavern: one hour.

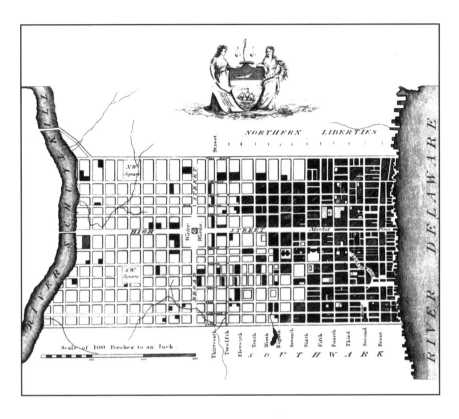

One of Penn's most important jobs was doling out land to new settlers. Penn had planned on 10,000 acres (4,000 hectacres) for his city, and he had sold that land to First Purchasers, colonists who had paid him ahead of time for this land. He had given his word that the best locations would go to First Purchasers who were already in the colony and ready to build. First Purchasers who had remained in England got the lesser lots.

Unfortunately, the amount of land planned didn't equal the amount of land available. Penn was

Philadelphia's square grid pattern became a model for cities throughout North America.

embarrassed that he could not fulfill his promise. Instead, First Purchasers had to settle for smaller lots, plus a plot of land in Northern Liberties, a suburb of the city that is now part of North Philadelphia, or in another part of the colony. Despite this oversight, building progressed rapidly. By June 1683, 80 houses stood completed. Near the city, 300 families had cleared land and started farms.

Next, Penn turned his attention to the local Lenni Lenape tribe. Although his representatives had met with the tribe, Penn had to follow up on his land purchase from the natives and negotiate a peace treaty. Negotiating a treaty was relatively easy for Penn. Unlike most colonial founders, Penn respected the rights of Indians. He had no intention of cheating, robbing, or killing them. He had sent a letter to the Lenni Lenape right after he gained his charter. Through his agent William Markham, Penn arranged a land purchase. Penn paid the

A number of native tribes lived in Pennsylvania when Penn's colonists arrived. Along the Delaware River, the primary culture was the Lenni Lenape. The Lenape were semi-nomadic, having separate winter and summer villages. Like many native people, they planted corn, beans, and squash—called the Three Sisters. The Susquehannas lived along the Susquehanna River in central Pennsylvania. The Mingo and Shawnee lived in western Pennsylvania. European diseases, such as smallpox, measles, and tuberculosis, killed off the populations of most Pennsylvania tribes.

Indians about £1,200 in cash and goods for 6,000 acres (2,400 hectares) of Pennsylvania land. Goods included wampum, guns, gunpowder, lead shot, rum, cloth, blankets, and coats.

Some colonial founders would have thought Penn's actions were ridiculous. If the king gave them the land, it was theirs. To them, native tribes had no say in colonists taking over the land, and they treated native people brutally. But Penn wanted his settlers to feel comfortable and for all Pennsylvanians to get along with the native people.

Penn met with the Lenni Lenape at Shackamaxon

A painting from the 1830s illustrates the meeting between Penn and the Lenni Lenape.

under a large, leafy elm tree. Penn and his men sat across from the tribal chief and his advisers. The Lenni Lenape gave Penn the name Onas, which was the Algonquian word for "pen" or "quill."

Together, the men negotiated the Great Treaty. Penn treated the natives with courtesy and fairness. For more than 70 years, Pennsylvanians and local natives lived in peace. It is possible that the Great Treaty was the only one between white men and natives that was neither sworn nor broken.

Penn's relations with the Indians were not without problems. There was a misunderstanding between the two cultures. The natives did not believe that anyone could own land. They accepted payment from the Europeans as "rent" for using the land. The Europeans, of course, expected that once money changed hands, they owned the property. Still, Penn tried to honor his agreements with the natives.

Penn had arranged peace with the natives, and the creation of Philadelphia was well under way. One problem, however, did not go away: the border dispute with Lord Baltimore.

Pennsylvania needed access to the Atlantic Ocean. Penn had planned his major city at the meeting point of the Delaware and Schuylkill rivers. Unfortunately, this spot was 40 miles (64 km) south of Pennsylvania's official border, according to the charter. At first, discussions between Penn's and

The Quaker meeting house and academy in Philadelphia

Lord Baltimore's agents went pleasantly. But as time wore on, tempers became frayed, honesty turned to fraud, and stubbornness prevented any solution to the problem. Penn's plan to be a good neighbor failed.

Lord Baltimore wanted his land back. He offered the opinion that Penn's Philadelphia was one of the prettiest towns … in *Maryland*. And he was serious. In 1684, Lord Baltimore headed back to England to argue his case before the king. William Penn was right behind him.

8 RETURNING TO ENGLAND

❧⳹⳾❧

William Penn was delighted to be back in England with his family. His newest son, William Jr., was almost 2 before he met his father. This was the second time the Penns used the name William for a son. Most families lost several children at a young age, and a child born later to the family was often given his sibling's name.

Within a year, Guli gave birth to another daughter, Gulielma Maria II. This child did not thrive. She died just after her fourth birthday.

At about this time, King Charles II died, and Penn's old friend the Duke of York became King James II. Penn visited and discussed religious tolerance with the new king. Through Penn's actions, more than 1,300 imprisoned Quakers were finally released from jail. However, the Quakers still suffered persecution for their religious beliefs. Quakers, noticeable by their clothing and their speech, were attacked on London streets and often chased by officials using dogs, guns, and whips. Despite Penn's efforts, some Quakers condemned him. His close friendship with the Roman Catholic king branded Penn as a traitor to the Quaker cause. He was even accused of being a Catholic priest in disguise.

Soon, Penn was in legal trouble again. King James II, who had been deposed in 1688, wrote to him from France, and the government seized the letter. The Privy Council—the advisers to the ruling king, William III—accused Penn of treason. Penn spoke on his own behalf, saying that he did indeed love King James II because James had been good to him and the Quakers. He said that to love someone only when they can be of value was false friendship. Penn pointed out that he

King James II, formerly the Duke of York (1633-1701)

couldn't possibly prevent James from writing to him, but that he, Penn, had no intention of trying to restore James to the throne. He was innocent.

Despite his plea, King William III and even some of Penn's powerful friends in the government believed he was guilty of plotting with the former king. He was arrested for treason, and once again had to answer charges against him. While waiting for the case to be resolved, Penn retired from public life, and he lost his governorship of Pennsylvania for two years. He wrote *Some Fruits of Solitude*, a collection of sayings and proverbs about life. In 1694, the government declared Penn innocent of all charges, and he was immediately reinstated as governor.

Also in 1694, Guli, Penn's beloved wife, died at age 50. Guli had always been sickly, and she had spent nearly eight months in bed. William Penn described her death as peaceful:

King James II admitted being a Catholic at a time when only the Protestant religion was accepted in England. He wanted to give Catholics powerful positions in the government and army. The House of Commons tried to control James, but he would not change his ways. In 1688, the House of Commons asked James' daughter Mary and her husband, William of Orange, to come to England from the Netherlands. William and Mary overthrew King James and took the throne. James II headed to France. This event was called the Glorious Revolution because it was a civil war without violence.

She quietly expired in my arms, her head upon my bosom, with a sensible and devout resignation of her soul to Almighty God. ... She was not only an excellent wife and mother, but an entire and constant friend ... an easy mistress and a good neighbor, especially to the poor.

Penn was grief-stricken. He wrote to his old friend Robert Turner:

Loving Friend, My extreme great affliction for the decease of my dear wife, makes me unfit to write much. ... In great peace and sweetness she departed, and to her gain, but our incomparable loss, being one of ten thousand, wise, chaste, humble, plain, modest, industrious, constant and undaunted, but God is God, and good—and so I hope ... not forsaken.

Penn's *Some Fruits of Solitude* is much like a list of proverbs from Ben Franklin. The thoughts are short tidbits of wisdom on many of life's topics. This collection was recently republished and is available in many libraries. Here is one of Penn's ideas, this one on virtue: "No one is forced to evil; only your consent make it yours."

Two years after Guli's death, Penn married Hannah Callowhill. Many Quaker leaders criticized him for his relationship with Hannah. He had started romancing her just eight months after Guli's death. Plus, Hannah was 25, while Penn was 52 years old, with three nearly

grown children. Also questionable in Quaker eyes was the fact that Hannah came with a large dowry from her wealthy merchant father. Nonetheless, the

The wedding of William Penn and Hannah Callowhill

Penns began producing children right away. Sadly, their first died before the baby was baptized and given a name. To add to their sadness, Penn's eldest son Springett, who was in his early 20s, died of an unknown illness.

Though still a teenager, Penn's son William Jr. married Mary Jones in 1698. The couple had three children, Gulielma Maria, Springett, and William III. But within just a few years, Mary died. William Jr. then married Lady Jenko Macpherson. Although he was a married man and a father, the younger William remained dependent on his own father for money. This, among other things, caused a serious split between father and son.

By 1699, Penn was eager to return to his colony, so he, Hannah, and Laetitia Penn left England to live in Pennsylvania. They headed for Pennsbury, the Penn family estate. Fifteen years had passed since Pennsbury had been finished, but this was the first time Penn had seen his home. The family spent two years in America, during which son John was born. For the rest of his life, John was called "the American" by the rest of the family.

During their time in America, the family was able to continue their life of luxury. Pennsylvania was a bustling, energetic colony. Businessmen exported lumber, furs, hemp, tobacco, iron, and copper. They imported British finished goods, such

as furniture, cloth, dishes, and silverware. Penn and his wife enjoyed the many items readily available in Philadelphia. Penn ordered bricks, lime, locks, nails, and some household goods. Hannah placed orders for chocolate, flour, bacon, coffee, and cornmeal. They set an excellent table and lived in great comfort while debts continued to mount.

Today, Pennsbury Manor is a museum dedicated to the life and times of William Penn.

Penn had business to tend to as well. He negotiated a treaty with the Susquehanna tribe to gain rights

*Penn signed
the Charter of
Privileges on
October 28,
1701, shortly
before he left
the colony
to return to
England.*

to the land they owned. Then in 1701, Penn was pressured by fellow Quakers to grant a new constitution, the Charter of Privileges, to the citizens of Pennsylvania. Among other things, the charter ensured freedom of religion for all Pennsylvania citizens. This document remained active until 1776 when it was replaced by a new state constitution. The success of religious freedom in Pennsylvania acted as a guide for similar freedoms outlined in the U.S. Constitution.

Penn and his family left Pennsylvania in October 1701. Although he did not know it at the time, he would never return. Heavy debts, poor health, and political problems would prevent him from leaving England again. As he left, he wrote:

So dear friends, my love again salutes you all, wishing that grace, mercy, and peace with all temporal blessings may abound richly among you. ... Your friend and lover in the Truth, William Penn.

Shortly after returning to Bristol, England, Hannah gave birth to her second son, Thomas. While delighted with the addition to his family, Penn was plagued by disputes with his colonists. With Penn in Europe, the Assembly in Pennsylvania had become feisty and quarrelsome. The colonists refused to pay rents owed to Penn if he wasn't there to collect them. Penn looked back with some irritation at his years of devotion to the colony. He recalled the thousands of pounds in taxes he had let go uncollected early in the colony's founding. And he remembered helping merchants set up shop and spending several thousand pounds of his own money to settle and maintain the colony.

Another problem he faced was the behavior of his son William Jr., who embarrassed his father with rebellious actions like drinking and gambling. Perhaps Penn didn't remember how his own behavior had shamed his father. When young William became involved in a tavern brawl in Philadelphia, it disgusted the Quakers in the colony. Penn simply didn't know how to deal with his son. They had always had a weak relationship.

Serious financial problems added to Penn's worries. In 1682, he had borrowed money from his steward, Philip Ford. When Penn didn't pay the debt, Ford added interest. By 1709, the original debt had more than quadrupled. Penn refused to pay, probably because he didn't have the money. It is also possible that Ford overcharged Penn, so the amount of the debt was questionable. When Penn didn't pay, he ended up in debtor's prison for nine months. Eventually, his friends paid part of the debt, and Penn got out of jail.

Soon more problems arose in the continuing dispute over the Pennsylvania/Maryland border. Lord Baltimore complained again, insisting that the border should be 40 miles (64 km) or so to the north. But Penn was in no condition to discuss any of this. His health was failing. He couldn't attend to the business of running his Irish and English estates, nor could he manage Pennsylvania from afar.

By 1712, Penn had to give up his responsibilities. He suffered several

The Pennsylvania/ Maryland border dispute continued until 1763, when Charles Mason and Jeremiah Dixon were hired to survey the land. By this time, Penn and Lord Baltimore were long dead. Mason and Dixon set a definite border between the two states, roughly 15 miles (24 km) south of Philadelphia. Few people know that Mason and Dixon's line also included the north-south boundary between Maryland and Delaware. The Mason-Dixon line, named for the two surveyors, is often used to mark the boundary between the North and the South.

small strokes that damaged his brain so much that he became childlike. He lost his memory and was so feeble, he couldn't even sign his own name without help. For the next six years, Penn would be sickly and unable to deal with business pressures.

Hannah took over running the Penn estates. The daughter of a button maker, she had experience in

Hannah Callowhill Penn in her later years

business and had no trouble managing her large family and the Penn property. Hannah became mother, nurse, manager, and proprietor of a colony. She cared for William as he aged and nursed her sons Tom and John through smallpox.

But managing the colony proved very difficult. Most men in the 1700s did not take kindly to following a woman's orders. The governor of Pennsylvania was a scoundrel and could not be relied on to run the colony fairly. Tenants continued to be difficult about paying rents, and Hannah struggled without the rent money. For her, the demands of being Mrs. Penn were many and the rewards far too few.

William Penn's grave sits among the graves of several of his children.

On July 30, 1718, William Penn awoke shivering with fever. It worsened through the day, and, at the age of 73, he died. He was buried beside his first wife, Gulielma, at the Quaker Meeting House at Jordans, near Chalfont St. Giles, England. He left his Irish and English estates to his son William Jr. Hannah and her children received Penn's land in Pennsylvania, as well as property in England. Sadly, Penn also left many debts behind him. But what was left in his will wasn't his only legacy. ❧

9 A LEGACY OF LIBERTY

❧❧❧

Often, famous men are average people who find themselves in extraordinary circumstances. William Penn was just such a man: a husband, a father, and a Quaker. He had great vision of an ideal future, but he was no saint. He was simply a man who tried his best.

Penn's best included the "City of Brotherly Love," Philadelphia. The city began as a center of manufacturing and shipping, and quickly grew to be one of the busiest ports in the colonies. When the first Continental Congress met in 1774, they chose Philadelphia for the meeting place. There, two years later, Thomas Jefferson wrote the Declaration of Independence, and John Hancock placed his large, fancy signature on the document. Philadelphia became the

A statue of William Penn tops the Philadelphia city hall.

In 1737, *Pennsylvanians agreed to buy more land from the Lenni Lenape in an agreement called the Walking Purchase. The agreement was to purchase an amount of land that could be covered by a day-and-a-half's walk. The price was agreed upon, and proprietary secretary James Logan hired men not to walk, but to run, in shifts. The natives expected the "walk" would be exactly that, the amount of land covered by one man walking alone. They believed they were cheated, and relations with the Pennsylvania Indians never improved after this shady deal.*

heart of American independence and freedom, and one of the early capitals of the United States.

Penn's treatment of all people was also admirable. He believed in treating everyone with kindness and courtesy. He did not limit his ideals to Quakers, Englishmen, or even whites. Penn's Great Treaty with the Lenni Lenape was unique in its fairness toward native people. The peace that came from Penn's dealings with them lasted until the Walking Purchase, an event typical of how white men treated natives.

But perhaps Penn's greatest legacy was founding a democratic government in Pennsylvania. People, he believed, had a God-given right to take part in their government. Citizens had the light of God within them that guided them to do good. That was the Quaker way. Good people chose good representatives, and those representatives would, Penn felt, pass good laws.

Penn's "Frame of Government" set down many of the rights and privileges Americans have fought for since the nation began. The Bill of Rights, amendments

that were attached to the U.S. Constitution in 1787, established freedoms of religion, press, and fair trials—all freedoms that appeared in Pennsylvania's early government.

Both the Declaration of Independence and the U.S. Constitution were created at Independence Hall in Philadelphia.

One of the most basic of those freedoms guaranteed to citizens of the United States is religious freedom. And because of Penn, the colony of Pennsylvania became the country's role model. Today, the state is still a home for Catholics, Jews, and Protestants, and a place where Amish, Dunkers, Mennonites, Moravian Brethren, and Schwenkfelders practice their religions as they have for more than 300 years.

Thanks to Penn, Pennsylvania-style justice was very different from justice in Europe and other

A statue of
William Penn
stands on the
grounds of
his beloved
Pennsbury
Manor.

English colonies. Leaders could not throw their
enemies in jail unless those enemies committed a
crime. Laws were clearly written, and punishments

were clearly defined. Defendants were entitled to jury trials. Penn knew from his own experience how much pressure could be used against juries. He wanted Pennsylvania juries to be free to weigh evidence and decide innocence and guilt based on that evidence. Today, American justice rests on the same foundations that Penn set up in Pennsylvania in 1682.

Penn's more than 50 written works remain as guidelines for moral living. They deal with family, friendships, religions, government, and moral behavior. In his book of proverbs and wise sayings, *Some Fruits of Solitude*, he wrote, "Love is above all, and when it prevails in us, we will be lovely, and in love with God and with one another." That was another of Penn's great gifts: a lifetime dedicated to loving friends. ✑

PENN'S LIFE

1665

Studies law in
Lincoln's Inn
then goes to
Ireland to manage
family estates

1667

Comes under
the influence of
Thomas Loe and
Quaker teachings

1644

Born October 14
in London

1650

1642

Isaac Newton, English
mathematician and
philosopher, is born

1655

Christian Huggens
discovers the rings
of Saturn

WORLD EVENTS

1670

Jailed for preaching on behalf of the Quakers; father dies

1672

Marries Gulielma Maria Springett

1675

Settles the estates of Edward Byllinge in present-day New Jersey

1670

1670

The Hudson's Bay Company is founded

1675-1676

King Philip's War is fought between the Wampanoag and British colonists in North America

PENN'S LIFE

1677

Embarks on a
missionary visit
to Europe with
George Fox

1681

Granted a charter
for present-day
Pennsylvania

1681-1682

Writes the first draft
of a constitution
for his new colony
and advertises sale
of land; goes to
Pennsylvania
without his family

1680

1681

The Canal du Midi, a
150-mile (240-km)
long canal in
southern France,
is finished after
eight years of work

WORLD EVENTS

1685

Secures the
release of 1,300
Quakers from
English prisons

1692-1694

Loses governorship
of Pennsylvania;
is cleared of
treason against the
English government;
Gulielma dies

1683

Pennsylvania's Frame
of Government is
established; Penn
supervises the survey
of Philadelphia

1690

1685

Johann Sebastian
Bach is born
in Germany

1692

Witchcraft trials
take place in Salem,
Massachusetts

1683

The French
royal court
moves to
Versailles

PENN'S LIFE

1696
Marries Hannah
Callowhill in
Bristol, England

1699
Returns to
Pennsylvania

1701
Grants a Charter
of Privileges to
Pennsylvania resi-
dents; Philadelphia
is incorporated
as a city

1700

1696
Denis Papin, a French
mathematician and
inventor, builds
two submarines

1703
Peter the Great
orders the building
of a new capital,
to be named
St. Petersburg

WORLD EVENTS

1718

Dies on July 30,
at Ruscombe,
Berkshire, England

1709

Goes to
debtor's prison

1712

Suffers a stroke

1720

1719

French scientist Rene
de Reaumur proposes
using wood to make
paper, which had
previously been made
from old cloth

1707

The Act of Union joins
Scotland, England, and
Wales into the United
Kingdom of Great Britain

DATE OF BIRTH: October 14, 1644

BIRTHPLACE: London, England

FATHER: Admiral Sir William Penn
(1621–1670)

MOTHER: Margaret Vanderschuren
(1622?–1682)

EDUCATION: Oxford University
Protestant Academy,
Saumur, France

FIRST SPOUSE: Gulielma Springett
(1644–1694)

DATE OF MARRIAGE: April 4, 1672

CHILDREN: Springett (1675–1696)
Laetitia (1677–1745)
William Jr. (1682–1720)
Gulielma (1685–1689)
Four died in infancy

SECOND SPOUSE: Hannah Callowhill
(1671–1727)

DATE OF MARRIAGE: March 5, 1696

CHILDREN: John (1700–1746)
Thomas (1702–1755)
Hannah (1703–1707)
Margaret (1704–1750)
Richard (1706–1771)
Dennis (1707–1722)
Hannah (1708–1709)

DATE OF DEATH: July 30, 1718

PLACE OF BURIAL: The Quaker House at
Jordans, England

FURTHER READING

Benge, Janet. *William Penn: Liberty and Justice for All*. Lynnwood, Wash.: Emerald Books, 2002.

Doherty, Kieran. *William Penn: Quaker Colonist*. Brookfield, Conn.: Millbrook Press, 1998.

Swain, Gwenyth. *Freedom Seeker: A Story About William Penn*. Minneapolis: Lerner Publishing, 2003.

Williams, Jean Kinney. *The Pennsylvania Colony*. Chanhassen, Minn.: The Child's World, 2004.

LOOK FOR MORE SIGNATURE LIVES BOOKS ABOUT THIS ERA:

Anne Hutchinson: *Puritan Protester*
ISBN 0-7565-1577-7

John Winthrop: *Colonial Governor of Massachusetts*
ISBN 0-7565-1591-2

Lord Baltimore: *Founder of Maryland*
ISBN 0-7565-1592-0

Roger Williams: *Founder of Rhode Island*
ISBN 0-7565-1596-3

On the Web

For more information on *William Penn*, use FactHound.

1. Go to *www.facthound.com*
2. Type in a search word related to this book or this book ID: 075651598X
3. Click on the *Fetch It* button.

FactHound will find Web sites related to this book.

Historic Sites

Pennsbury Manor
400 Pennsbury Memorial Road
Morrisville, PA 19067
215/946-0400
William Penn's home, located just outside Philadelphia

The Historical Society of Pennsylvania
1300 Locust St.
Philadelphia, PA 19107
215/732-6200
Collections and exhibits dating back to colonial times

bailiff
a court usher, clerk, or other official

bankrupt
unable to pay debts

chamber pot
a type of bowl that people used as a toilet

conspiring
plotting to commit a crime

conversion
the changing to or accepting of a different religion
as one's own faith

defendants
in trials, the accused criminals

epidemics
uncontrolled diseases, such as smallpox or the
plague, that attack a large number of people

guineas
British coins used prior to 1971; one is equal to
one pound plus one shilling

precedent
an example for future events

sects
religious groups, such as Mennonites or Quakers

shipwrights
carpenters who build or repair ships

steward
a person who manages another's finances

tolerance
the acceptance of people's beliefs or actions that
differ from one's own beliefs or actions

Chapter 1

Page 12, line 11: "Penn, William," *Literary Encyclopedia*. 1 February 2005. www.litencyc.com/php/speople.php?rec=true&UID=4986.

Page 15, sidebar: Kieran Doherty. *William Penn: Quaker Colonist*. Brookfield, Conn.: Millbrook Press, 1998, p. 105.

Chapter 2

Page 25, line 9: "William Penn—Early Life." 5 January 2005. www.2020site. org/penn/earlylife.html.

Chapter 4

Page 36, line 26: Jim Powell. "William Penn—America's First Great Champion for Liberty and Peace." 1 February 2005. www.fee.org/vnes.php?nid=3309&pr intable=Y.

Page 37, line 6: William Penn. "William Penn Quotes," 27 March 2005. www. brainyquote.com/quotes/autheros/w/william_penn.html.

Page 40, line 1: Elizabeth Gray Vining. *Penn*. Philadelphia: Philadelphia Yearly Meeting of the Religious Society of Friends, 1986, p. 139.

Chapter 5

Page 43, line 15: Samuel M. Janney. *The Life of William Penn; with Selections from his Correspondence and Auto-biography*. Freeport, N.Y.: Books for Libraries Press, 1977, p. 89.

Page 47, line 1: Henry William Elson. *History of the United States of America*. New York: MacMillan Company, 1904. 14 October 2005. http://www. usgennet.org/usa/topic/colonial/book/chap7_3.html#1.

Page 52, line 19: *The Life of William Penn; with Selections from his Correspondence and Auto-biography*, p. 156.

Chapter 6

Page 57, line 4: "William Penn—America's First Great Champion for Liberty and Peace."

Page 58, line 3: Bill Samuel. "William Penn." 27 March 2005. www.quakerinfo. com/quakpenn.shtml.

Page 64, line 15: Jean R. Soderlund. *William Penn and the Founding of Pennsylvania*. Philadelphia: University of Pennsylvania Press, 1983, p. 165.

Page 65, line 1: Ibid, p. 171.

Chapter 7

Page 70, line 21: "William Penn in Pennsylvania," 5 January 2005. www.dep.state.pa.us/dep/PA_Env-Her/William_Penn.htm.

Chapter 8

Page 80, line 1: Alfred T. Story. "The Grave of William Penn." *Harper's Magazine*, 1881. 9 September 2005. http://freepages.history.roostweb.com/~amxroads/Penn.

Page 80, line 10: *The Life of William Penn; with Selections from his Correspondence and Auto-biography*, p. 378.

Page 80, sidebar: William Penn. *Some Fruits of Solitude*. Scottdale, Pa.: Herald Press, 2003, p. 104.

Page 85, line 1: *The Life of William Penn; with Selections from his Correspondence and Auto-biography*, p. 396.

Beatty, Edward Corbyn Obert. *William Penn as Social Philosopher*. New York: Columbia University Press, 1939.

Bronner, Edwin B. *Penn's "Holy Experiment:" The Founding of Pennsylvania 1681–1701*. New York: Temple University Publications, 1962.

Illick, Joseph E. *William Penn, the Politician: His Relations with the English Government*. Ithaca, N.Y.: Cornell University Press, 1965.

Janney, Samuel M. *The Life of William Penn; with Selections from his Correspondence and Auto-biography*. Freeport, N.Y.: Books for Libraries Press, 1977.

Nash, Gary B. *Quakers and Politics: Pennsylvania, 1681–1726*. Princeton, N.J.: Princeton University Press, 1968.

"Penn Family, Part 1." 9 September 2005. www.csm.uwe.ac.uk/~rstephen/livingeaston/local_history/Penn/Penn_family_part_1.html.

Penn, William. "Quotations from William Penn." 27 March 2005. www.gwyneddfriends.org/wmpenn.htm#quotes.

Penn, William. *Some Fruits of Solitude*. Scottdale, Pa.: Herald Press, 2003.

Powell, Jim. "William Penn—America's First Great Champion for Liberty and Peace." 1 February 2005. www.fee.org/vnews.php?nid=3309.

Samuel, Bill. "William Penn." 27 March 2005. www.quakerinfo.com/quakpenn.shtml.

Soderlund, Jean R. *William Penn and the Founding of Pennsylvania*. Philadelphia: University of Pennsylvania Press, 1983.

"Trial of William Penn." 5 January 2005. http://tarlton.law.utexas.edu/lpop/etext/penntrial.html.

Vining, Elizabeth Gray. *Penn*. Philadelphia: Philadelphia Yearly Meeting of the Religious Society of Friends, 1986.

"William Penn—Early Life." 5 January 2005. www.2020site.org/penn/earlylife.html.

"William Penn in Pennsylvania." 5 January 2005. www.dep.state.pa.us/dep/PA_Env-Her/William_Penn.htm.

Barbara A. Somervill has been writing for more than 30 years. She has written newspaper and magazine articles, video scripts, and books for children. She enjoys writing about science and investigating people's lives for biographies. She is an avid reader and traveler. Ms. Somervill lives with her husband in South Carolina.